How to Play HAWAIIAN ʻUKULELE for Kids

Michael Preston

Mutual Publishing

Library of Congress Control Number: 2023943248

ISBN: 978-1-949307-55-9

Drawings by Natalie Hajdu on pg. 5, 16, 17, 49, 50
Design by Courtney Tomasu

First Printing, November 2023

Mutual Publishing, LLC
1215 Center Street, Suite 210
Honolulu, Hawaii 96816
Ph: 808-732-1709 / Fax: 808-734-4094
email: info@mutualpublishing.com
www.mutualpublishing.com

Printed in South Korea

Images from Dreamstime.com: pg. 2 (boy) © Panom Pensawang; pg. 3 (girl) © Aekkorn Poomseetana; pg. 4 © Lufimorgan; pg. 5 (cowrie shells) © Aray3900; pg. 6 (top girl) © Kittichai Boonpong, pg. 23 (boy) © Olesia Bilkei; pg. 8 © Navee Sangvitoon; pg. 12, (ʻukulele) © Siiixth; pg. 33 (monk seal) © Slowmotiongli; pg. 37 (boy) © Kostiantyn Gerashchenk; pg. 54 (ʻukulele with tuner) © 9george, (boy) © Sutthinon Sanyakup; cover (girl) © Woraphon Banchobdi, (boy) © Dmitry Molchanov

Images from Wikimedia.com: pg. 9 (Amahiki) © Alan Schmierer, (nēnē) © Frederick Frohawk, (Pacific Golden Plover) © Naumann; pg. 10 (map) © Central Intelligence Agency; pg. 15 (nēnē) © J. Wei; pg. 30 (pueo), 55 (pueo) © HarmonyonPlanetEarth; pg. 39 (honu) © Ali Bayless/NOAA; pg. 40 (Kōlea) © JJ Harrison; pg. 42 (dolphin) © Alexia Pihier for MDC SeaMarc Maldives; pg. 55 (nēnē) © Jörg Hempel, (kōlea) © Daniel Ramirez, (monk seal) © Ed Lyman/NOAA, under Permit #15240, (naiʻa) © Claire Fackler/ NOAA

Images from FreePik.com: pg. 1, 23 (girl singing icon), 28, 30, 32, 35, 42, 44 (background), cover (floral backgound) © freepik; pg. 2 (musical notes), 23 (background), cover (muscial splotch) © brgfx; pg. 5 (musical notes) © macrovector, (honu) © wirestock; pg. 6 (musical instruments) © Museu Cavaquinho; pg. 21 © kjpargeter; pg. 24 (hands clapping) © upklyak; pg. 25 (background) © brgfx; pg. 29 (background) © Art.shcherbyna; pg. 36 (background) © rawpixel.com; pg. 26, 38, 40, 46 (background) © pikisuperstar; pg. 43 (happy faces) © Harryarts; pg. 44 (shiba inu) © catalyststuff; cover (ocean background) © frimufilms

Images from Hawaiʻi State Archives: pg. 7 (Queen Liliʻuokalani and King Kalākaua); pg. 11 (King Kalākaua); pg. 47 (Queen Liliʻuokalani)

Image from iStockphoto.com: pg. 10 (map) © bogdanserban

Images from flaticon.com: pg. 19 (check mark and X) © roundicons

Contents

Acknowledgments

Warmest thanks to **Keola Beamer** for so kindly granting permission to include a verse from the song, "Pūpū Hinuhinu." As a composer, teacher, and slack-key guitar player, Keola is a long-time legend in Hawai'i. His mother, Winona, composed this sweet song about seashells. Young children in Hawaiian schools delight in performing this song with simple hula movement.

Much gratitude also goes out to **Tria** (Trisha Cabral) who has composed many children's songs in her island home of Maui. They can be heard on her CD entitled *Honu: Island Melodies for Kids.* Tria very kindly allowed us to use the first verse of her delightful song "Honu," about the Hawaiian green sea turtle.

Both musicians were open-hearted and kind in responding to our request to use their music for this book. Those who live, or have lived, in Hawai'i keep in their hearts the warmth of such aloha.

Many thanks go to the artists and editors at Mutual Publishing who have consistently created books of high quality over the years and who have published many 'ukulele instruction books over the years.

Special thanks to Jane Gillespie of Mutual Publishing for her clarity, patience, and editorial skills, and to Courtney Tomasu for her graphic artistry.

Introduction

There are many books that teach adults and older children how to play the 'ukulele, but not many for young children between five and nine years old (kindergarten through early elementary grades). *How to Play the Hawaiian 'Ukulele for Kids* is specifically for beginners who are picking up the 'ukulele for the first time.

Although the 'ukulele has spread all over the world and is often used by famous performers, it first **originated** in Hawai'i. It could be considered the ambassador instrument of the Hawaiian islands!

From left: Hawaiian 'ukulele, Madeira braguinha, Portuguese cavaquinho, Brazilian cavaquinho, Cape Verde cavaquinho.

The book begins with the story of how Polynesians first came to these islands and celebrated nature and its beauty. Much later, Portuguese settlers brought to Hawai'i a small, stringed instrument called the *braguinha.* People were fascinated by its sound and by the skill of the players. With encouragement from King Kalākaua, very similar instruments named 'ukuleles, began to be fashioned out of beautiful Hawaiian wood such as koa.

Although some of the best 'ukulele performers can pick out melodies, most players learn chords and sing and strum in rhythm to different songs.

Included are well-known songs of early childhood with new lyrics that introduce children to the some of the unique birds and sea creatures of the Hawaiian Islands. **In small, easy steps,** young children will learn how to play the chords that go with these tunes.

Three songs in this book are unique to Hawai'i. The first is Winona Beamer's much-loved song of Hawaiian sea shells, named "Pūpū Hinuhinu." Her son, Keola Beamer, a very well-known, slack key guitarist, generously gave permission to include her song! To really appreciate how this song fits into nature, a link to a YouTube is included. Its rendering is very child-friendly and also has children performing along with the singer.

Queen Lili'uokalani

Another lovely song was composed by a young musician on Maui named Tria who has her own book of children's songs. Her song is about the Hawaiian green sea turtle, known in Hawaiian as honu.

Tria very kindly gave permission to include the first verse of her "Honu" song. There is a lovely 'ukulele accompaniment version on YouTube (link is included), and after learning the first verse in this book, your child will be able to play along with the other verses.

The chorus to "Aloha 'Oe" by Hawai'i's beloved Queen Lili'uokalani is introduced, along with a very simple 'ukulele rendition available on YouTube.

King Kalākaua

Other songs include the well-known tune of "Old King Cole" which has been adapted as a tribute to Hawai'i's King Kālakaua, who was known as the Merrie Monarch because of his love of music and hula. The annual Merrie Monarch Festival on Hawai'i Island (the Big Island) is named in his honor. The main avenue through Waikīkī is named after King Kalākaua. He was responsible for encouraging the craftsmanship and popularity of a uniquely local Hawaiian instrument that has now spread all over the world!

The 'ukulele is travel-friendly, sturdy for kids to handle, and so much fun to play with others—before long, your child will be able to join in any impromptu, backyard kanikapila (musical jam

session). Included is the ubiquitous "Happy Birthday" song so your child can sing and play for mom or dad, brothers, sisters, relatives, and friends at any and every birthday party!

☆ **If your child, or you, want to go further** with learning 'ukulele, pick up a copy of *Hawaiian 'Ukulele: Keys, Chords, and Strums for Beginners* and *Learn the Hawaiian 'Ukulele.* They will take a beginner to intermediate level.

Have fun and keep playing!

Michael Preston

A Note to Parents, Grandparents, Guides, and Teachers

Younger children will need help in understanding new steps—especially at the beginning.

This book can be a wonderful opportunity and journey to learn to play 'ukulele together!

Hawai'i Amakihi, Hakalau Forest National Wildlife Refuge.

Hawai'i Before the First People

Long before the first people arrived in Hawai'i by canoe, the forests knew the sound of wind, rushing waterfalls, and beautiful birdsongs. The little kōlea ran along the beach and the nēnē goose, like the sailors, journeyed from far away to live in the islands of Hawai'i.

Nēnē.

Pacific Golden Plover.

First People Sail to Hawai'i

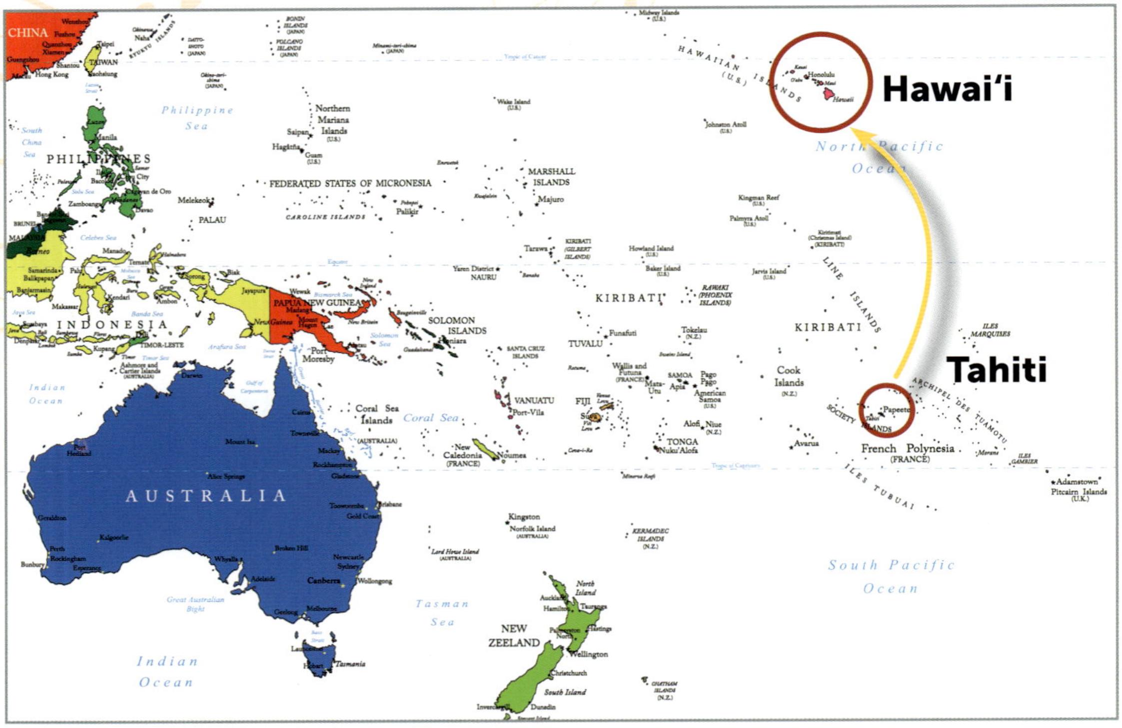

The first people from Kahiki (Tahiti) sailed to Hawai'i. They sang songs of their journey, and soon many songs about their lives in Hawai'i.

Much later, new sailors arrived on ships bringing small musical instruments with strings. Some of the Hawaiians thought the way their fingers jumped on the strings looked like dancing fleas! They called this instrument a flea ('uku) which dances (lele). To this day, it has kept its name—'ukulele!

'Ukulele Becomes Part of Hawaiian Family

The 'ukulele became very popular. It was played in almost every singing group.

King Kalākaua, known as the Merrie Monarch, loved music and he wanted 'ukuleles to be made and played all over the islands.

Ever since, from his time to today, all types of 'ukulele have been made, many out of lovely Hawaiian woods such as koa.

'Ukuleles come in many sizes. The most common ones are called **Soprano** 'ukuleles. They are the smallest and best for children. But there are also **Concert** and **Tenor** 'ukuleles that are bigger. For adults, or people with bigger hands, they are often the best choice.

King Kalākaua

The five main members of the 'ukulele family, from left to right: standard or soprano 'ukulele, concert 'ukulele, tenor 'ukulele, six-string 'ukulele, and eight-string 'ukulele.

'Ukulele Parts

'Ukuleles, big or small, are all made of the same parts.

An 'ukulele is a bit like a person. It has a head, a long neck, a chest, and a belly.

It doesn't need legs because we hold it and carry it!

The top is called the **head**. It has four pegs called tuners. These tighten the strings to tune them. (See next page about tuning.)

The **neck** has many frets where you press down on the different strings to make chords.

The **body**, which is like a chest and a belly, helps to make the sound mellow and beautiful and lets the 'ukulele's voice sing out of the **sound hole.**

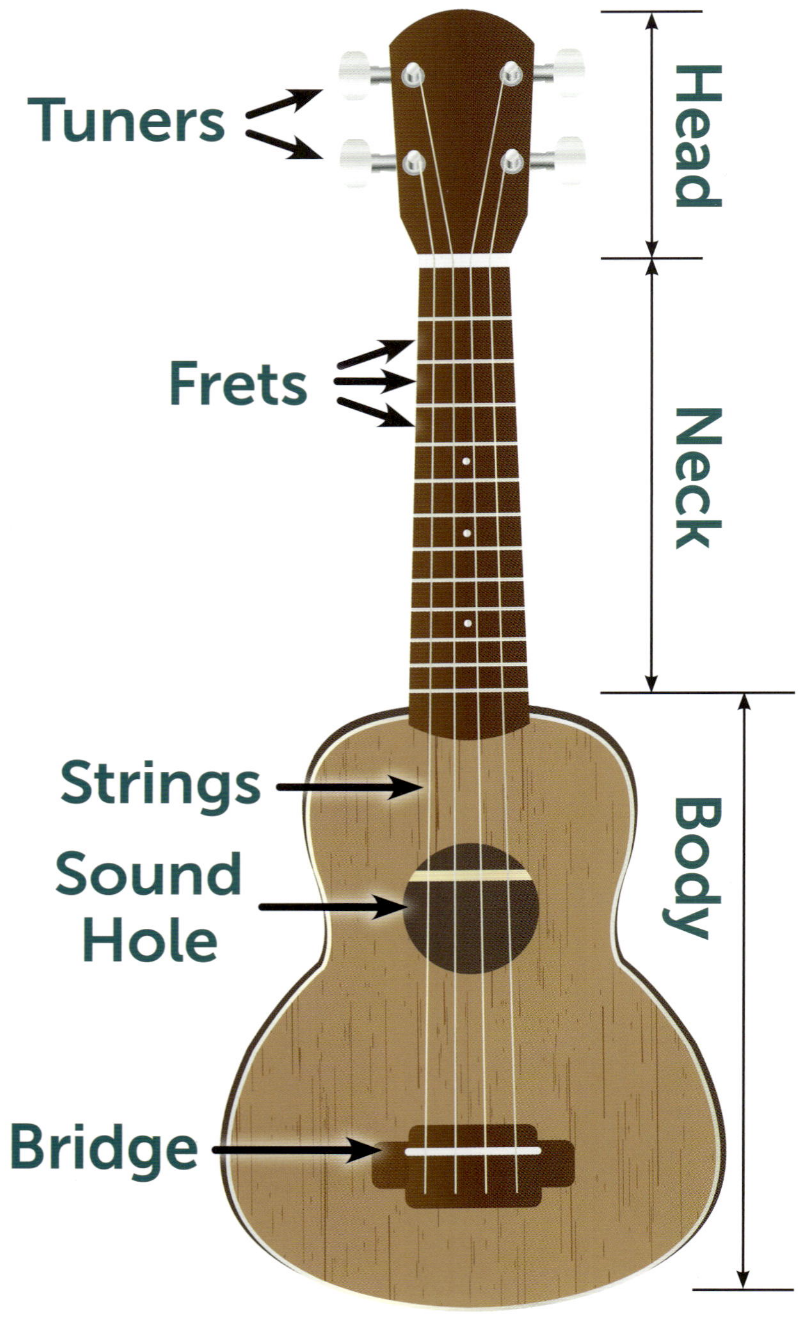

Holding Your 'Ukulele

There are two ways to hold your 'ukulele for playing—sitting or standing.

Sitting

You can play sitting down or even cross-legged on the floor. The curved bottom of the sound box can rest on your thigh and your right hand above the sound hole.

The thumb of your left hand can either rest under the neck of the 'ukulele or come round a little.

Standing

If you want to stand, you should hold your 'ukulele about halfway down your chest, on your right. Tuck you left elbow in a little, but not too tightly! Your right hand should be above the sound hole or a little towards the neck. Your left hand holds the neck of the 'ukulele with fingers ready to play!

The Names of the Four Strings of Your 'Ukulele

The four strings are tuned to **G C E A**

They are also numbered

4th G
3rd C
2nd E
1st A

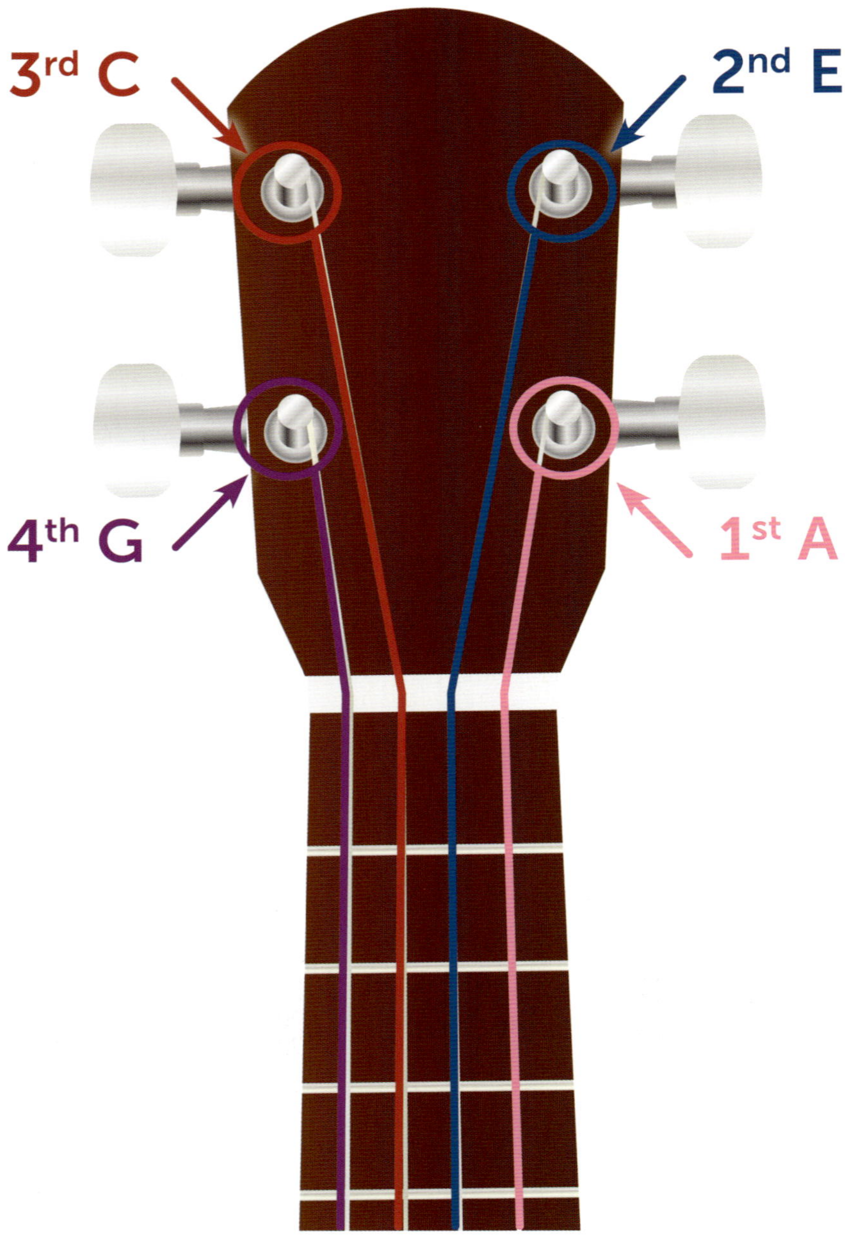

The next page explains how to tune each string!

Tuning Your 'Ukulele

The Nēnē (neh-neh) Goose is Hawai'i's State Bird

Once you know the tune, sing and tune each string in order:

Goose Calls Ee Ay

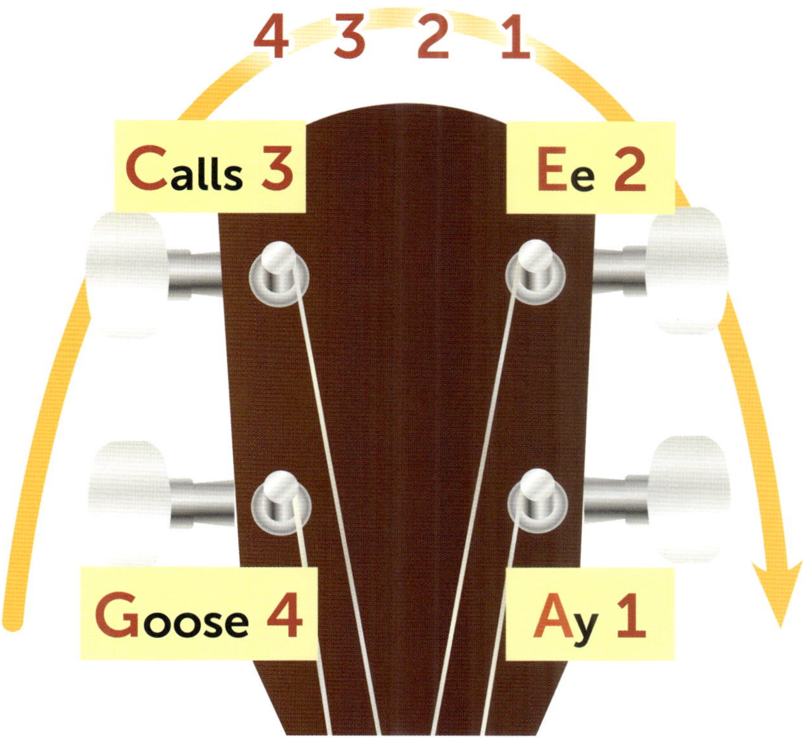

Tune

- 4 G (Goose)
- 3 C (Calls)
- 2 E (Ee)
- 1 A (Ay)

Tuning on the piano or keyboard

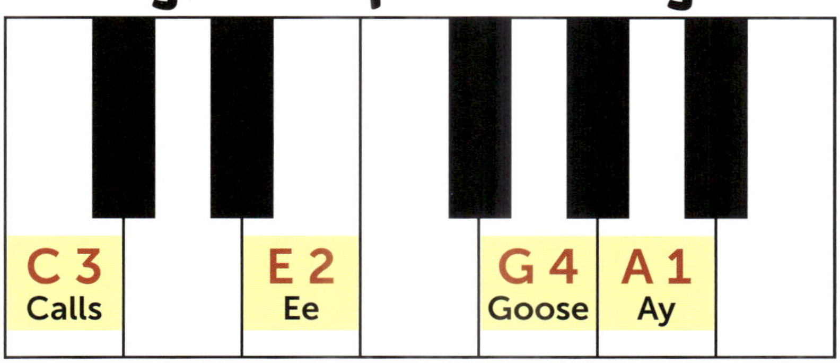

(If electronic tuning is needed, see page 54.)

Practice Smooth Down and Up Strums

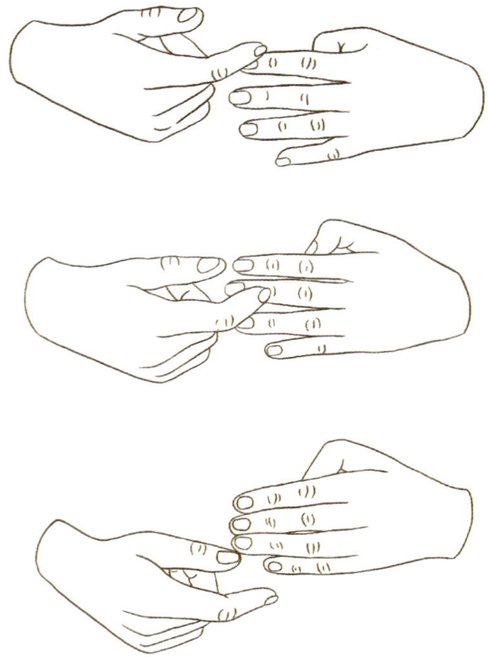

All our ʻukulele tunes will be made of **down** and **up** strums!

Let's learn how to strum. Hold your left hand in front of your chest and pretend that your hand is the ʻukulele and your fingers are the strings. With your right hand, gently drag your pointer finger down your left hand fingers, like the examples to the right.

Strum so your pointer finger **slowly rolls** over each finger of your left hand.

At first, only strum down: **Say and Strum Down**

Down-strum **Down-strum** **Down-strum** **Down-strum**

Once you have done this smoothly a few times—

Now you can try the Up-strum: **Say and Strum Up**

Up-strum **Up-strum** **Up-strum** **Up-strum**

Do this a few times.

Notice when you strum **down** your pointer's **fingernail** and **fingertip** are rolling over your left hand fingers.

When you strum **up**, just your **fingertip** is rolling over your left hand fingers.

Now practice **down** and **up** strums!

To help you remember good strumming with the correct part of you finger, practice like this.

When your finger goes **down** say, "**Nail**!"

Four times **down** would be **Nail** **Nail** **Nail** **Nail**

Four times **up** would be **Finger** **Finger** **Finger** **Finger**

Now practice this simple pattern!

Nail **Finger** **Nail** **Finger** **Nail** **Finger** **Nail** **Finger**

Now practice this same strum **down**-**up** on your 'ukulele strings—just above the sound hole, like this:

Strumming on Your 'Ukulele

Put your right (strumming) hand over the sound hole, or a little further up, to where it feels comfortable.

Your right hand must be very relaxed!

No stiff fingers, everything should be floppy!

Curl your fingers up like the pictures above and below show, with JUST your first finger or pointer sticking out and a little curved.

This is all you use to strum with!

When you strum **down**, you mostly use your fingernail.

When you strum **up**, you use the pad of your finger.

Strum **DOWN** using mostly your fingernail.

Strum **UP** with the soft part of your fingertip.

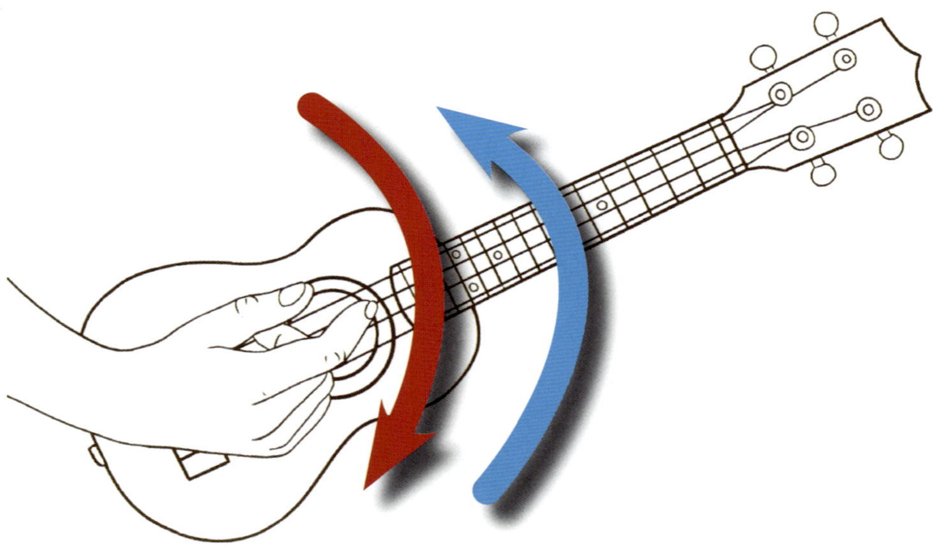

Using Your Left Hand to Make Chords and Notes

Your left hand is very important in ‘ukulele playing!

First, you need to support the other end of your ‘ukulele. The space between your thumb and the rest of your hand is where you do this. Your thumb can stick up a bit, but don’t curl it round to touch the 4th string. (This is too much!)

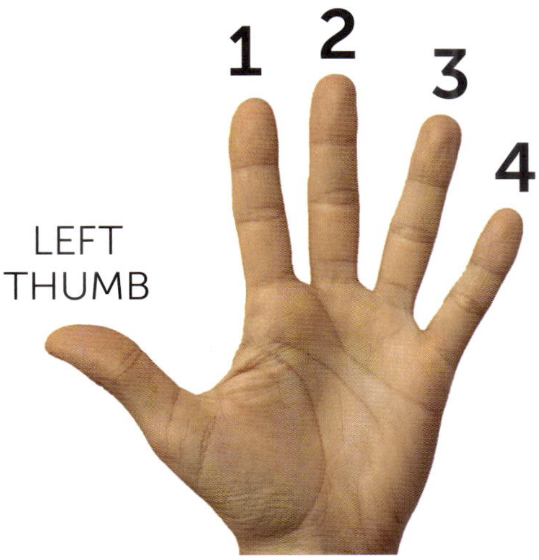

The four fingers of your hand are numbered as in the picture to the left.

This will help you to know later which finger goes in which place.

When you learn new chords to accompany the songs, you will see a picture like the ones below, with its name and small colored circles on the strings with the finger number on each.

Some chords like this one, are easy to learn and play. Some chords are a little more difficult and you will have to practice more and strengthen your finger grip!

Chord of F

F

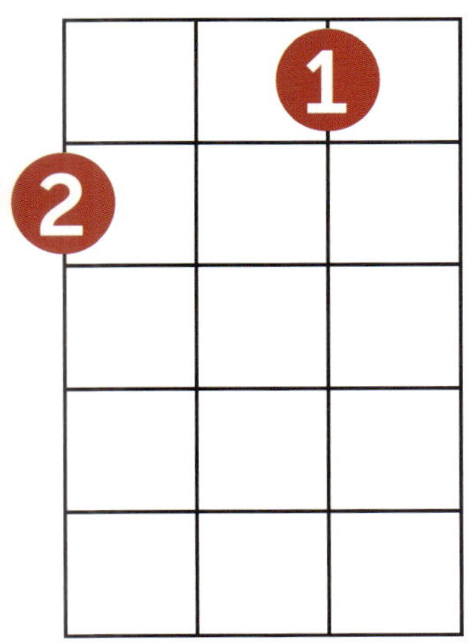

Chords and Their Friends

The first chord you will learn is the **C chord** and soon after, two regular friends—the **F chord** and the **G^7 chord**.

They are part of the family of C, because they often help each other in playing a song!

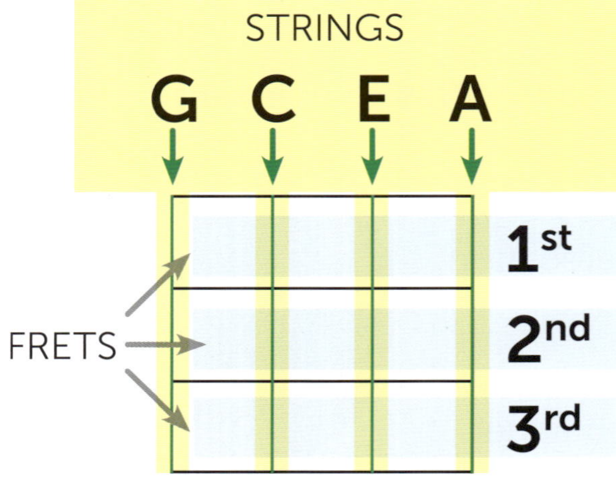

Before we start, here is a picture to show you again the strings' names—**G C E A**

And also the frets (spaces between the fret wires).

Here is the **C chord.**

Put your 3rd finger on the 1st string and on the 3rd fret.

Now gently strum. There should be a clear sound. To check you are pressing right, try plucking just the string you are pressing to hear that it sounds clear. Then, if it does, go back to strumming for our first song!

C Chord, Down-strum

Strum the **C chord** for each down arrow and sing the words.

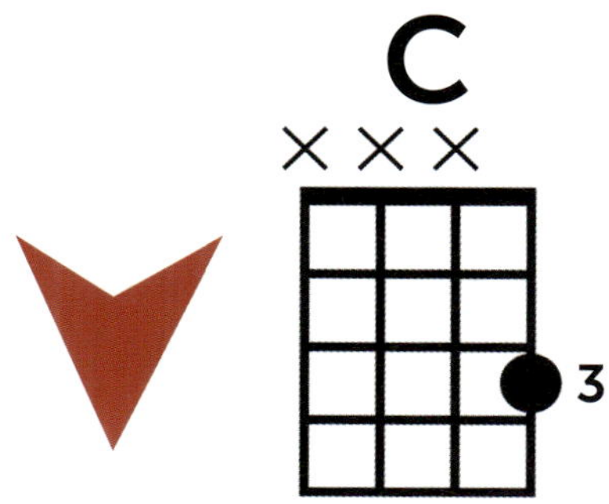

C	Chord	Down	Strum
C	Chord	Down	Strum
C	Chord	Down	Strum
C	Chord	Down	Down
Strum	Strum	Strum	Strum

The Three Main Chords of the C Family

Practice playing these chords and changing to the next one smoothly.

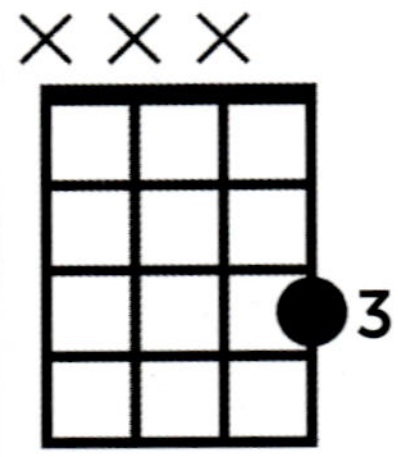

C chord STRUM DOWN EIGHT TIMES

C - two - three - four - five - six - seven - eight

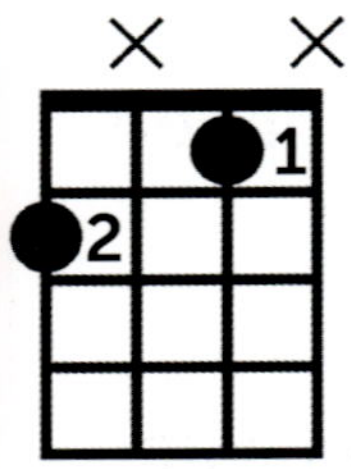

F chord STRUM DOWN EIGHT TIMES

F - two - three - four - five - six - seven - eight

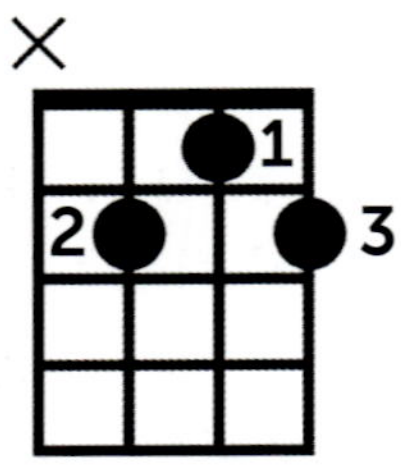

G^7 chord STRUM DOWN EIGHT TIMES

G^7 - two - three - four - five - six - seven - eight

Challenge! Once you can do this, try strumming each chord six times, then four times, then three times, then two times, and finally strum each chord once and smoothly change to the next one. If you can do this, it shows you really know this family of chords and can easily use them in any song!

Helpful Hint: How to Start a Song on the Right Note

When you strum the chords of any song in this book, you can usually **feel** what note to start singing on. But if you are not sure, here is how to find the note.

Before you start strumming the C chord for **"Twinkle, Twinkle, Little Star,"** you can check the **starting note** this way. You will see a little a **box** ▭ with the name of the note, and an arrow pointing to the exact string. Just pluck that string. (It is called an **open string** because no fingers are pressing on it). This is the note to begin the song.

Some songs do not start with a note made by an open string**. You have to press down with one finger on a particular place.** For these songs, you will see a **circle** ◯ with the name of the note and an arrow pointing to where you have to press down. The "Happy Birthday Song" starts on the note D. Press your 2nd finger down on this exact place (indicated by the red dot) and pluck the string. **This is the note to start singing with.** Now you can start strumming and singing the song!

Strumming for Long Notes

Often the **last** word in a part of a song needs **more than one strum.**

Before you play "Twinkle,Twinkle, Little Star," look at how you need to add **extra strums** at the end of some lines.

You can find out by clapping for each part of the words

(one clap for each part of the word)

Twin – kle, twin – kle

At the end of the next line, you have to clap twice on "star."

Sing it and clap, you will see!

Lit – tle star ———— ("star" is longer and needs two claps)

This is just the same with strums!

In all of the songs that you will learn, if you see two strums under a word, it is because if you were clapping it would need more claps.

Long words are almost always at the **<u>end</u>** of a line!

Now try strumming and singing "Twinkle, Twinkle, Little Star" on the next page.

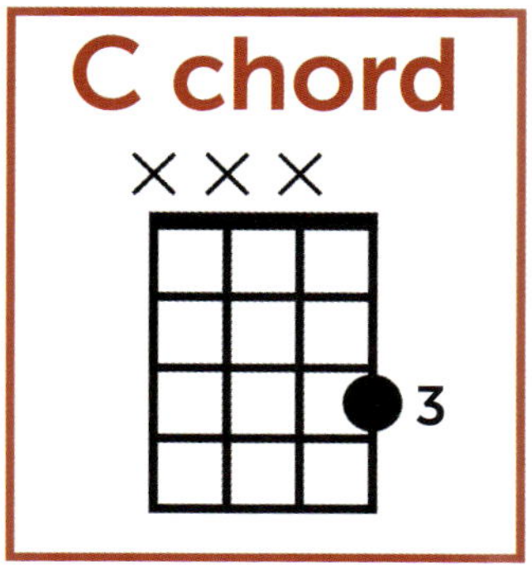

Twinkle, Twinkle, Little Star

Strum down once for each chord symbol.

C C C C
Twin - kle Twin - kle

F F C C
Lit - tle Star

F F C C
How I Won - der

G7 G7 C C
What You Are !

C chord

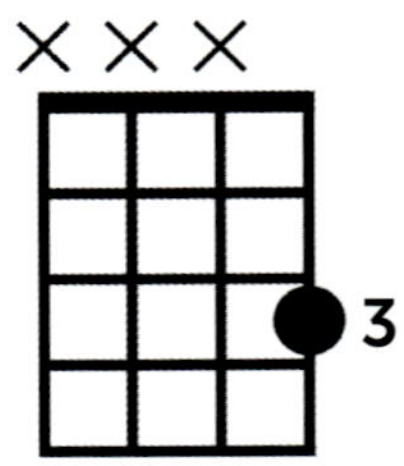

F chord

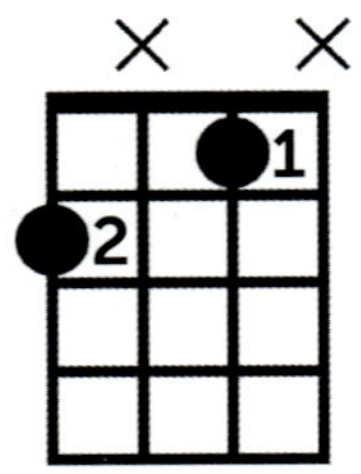

G7 chord

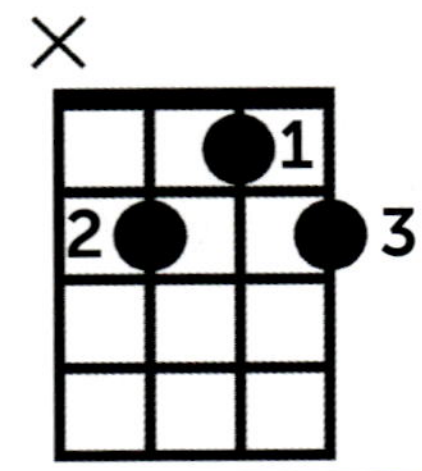

Nēnē Calling

(Sing to the tune of "Twinkle, Twinkle, Little Star")

Strum down once for each chord symbol.

C C C C
Nē - nē, Nē - nē

F F C C
Bird so free!

F F C C
Call - ing, Call - ing,

G^7 G^7 C C
Out to me!

C C F F
Watch - ing from the

C C G7 G7
Cliffs so high,

C C F F
Fly - ing, up - wards

F F G7 G7
In the sky *(repeat from the start of song)*

Adding and Playing the C^7 Chord

1st finger on 1st string and on the 1st fret.

This is one of the easiest chords! Practice strumming this way:

Down-strum F the F chord 8 times in each line.

F F F F F F F F

F - two - three - four - five - six - seven - eight

Now the C^7 chord the same way!

C^7 C^7 C^7 C^7 C^7 C^7 C^7 C^7

C^7 - two - three - four - five - six - seven - eight

Now back to the F chord!

F F F F F F F F

F - two - three - four - five - six - seven - eight

Strumming Chords Down and Up

It is time to learn to strum **DOWN** ▼ and **UP**. △

When you strum chords like the last page, just sing the word and in between. So, on each **NUMBER** or **CHORD** strum **down** (the triangle points down) ▼

For each word **AND** strum **up** (the triangle points up) △

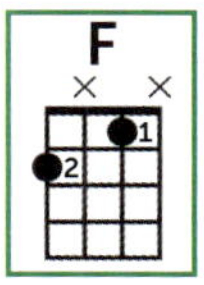

Hold the F chord and practice strumming it down and up.

Sing like this:

F and 2 and 3 and 4 and 5 and 6 and 7 and 8

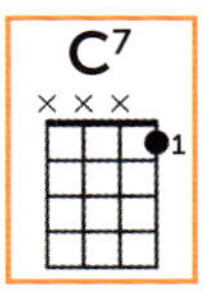

Now add the C^7 chord strumming the same way.

C^7 and 2 and 3 and 4 and 5 and 6 and 7 and 8

And finish by strumming the F chord down and up.

F and 2 and 3 and 4 and 5 and 6 and 7 and 8

Pueo Song

(Sing to the tune of "Hot Cross Buns")

F chord

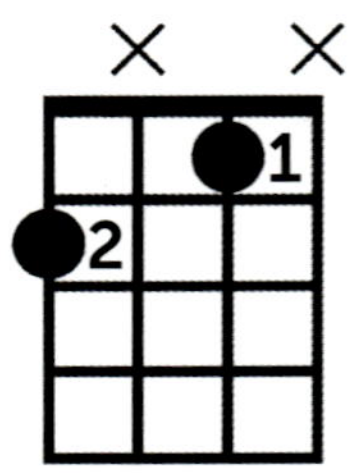

F Strum down

F Strum up

C^7 chord

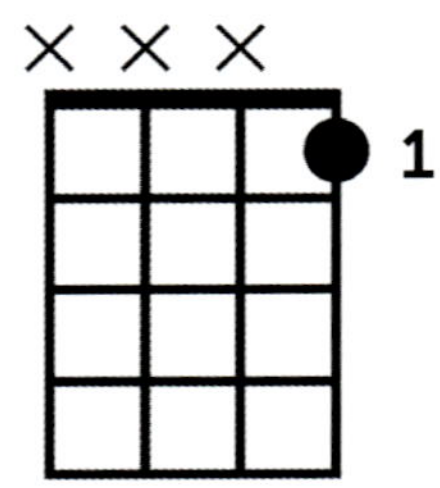

C^7 Strum down

C^7 Strum up

F C^7 F F F C^7 F F

Pu— e— o—— Pu— e— o——

F F(up) F F(up)

Watch - ing lit - tle

C^7 C^7(up) C^7 C^7(up)

Creat - ures scur - ry

F C^7 F F

To and fro — !

Playing the G chord

Practice the chords of the C Family with a new chord—G.

You already know the C and G^7 chord. Now we will add a new chord—**G**—just a little different from the G^7

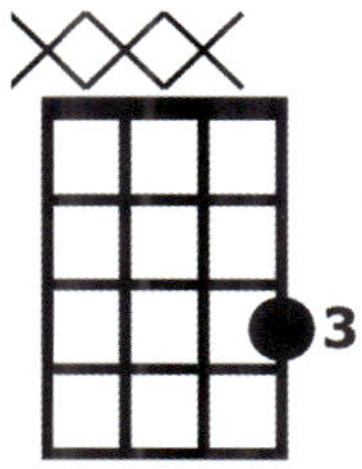

C chord STRUM DOWN EIGHT TIMES

C C C C C C C C

C - **two** - **three** - **four** - **five** - **six** - **seven** - **eight**

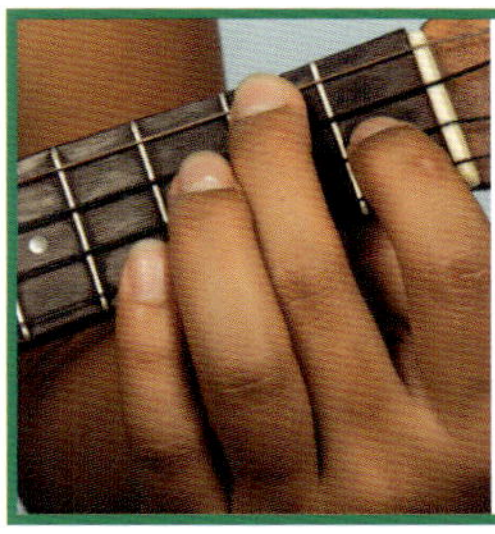

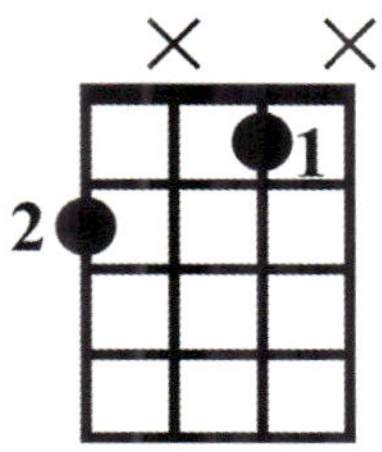

F chord STRUM DOWN EIGHT TIMES

F F F F F F F F

F - **two** - **three** - **four** - **five** - **six** - **seven** - **eight**

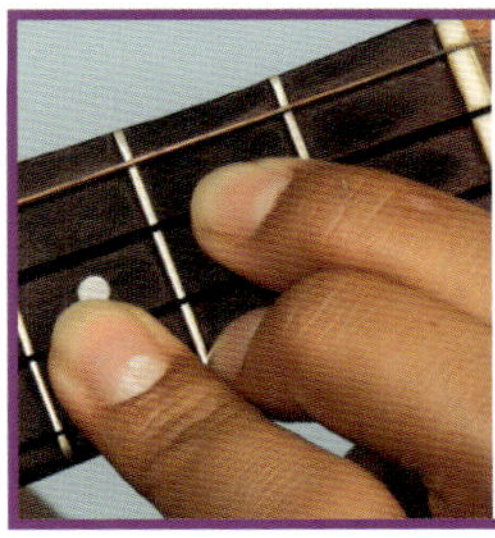

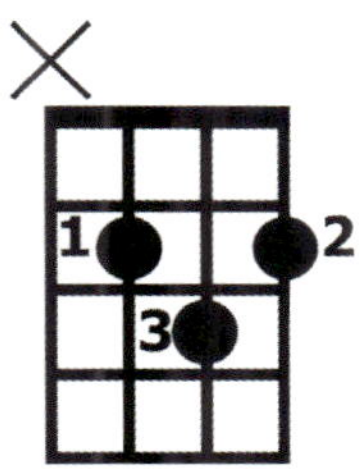

G chord STRUM DOWN EIGHT TIMES

G G G G G G G G

G - **two** - **three** - **four** - **five** - **six** - **seven** - **eight**

Challenge! Once you can do this, try strumming each chord six times, then four times, then three times, then two times, and finally strum each chord once and smoothly change to the next one. If you can do this, it shows you really know this family of chords and can easily use them in any song!

Hawaiian Monk Seal Song

(Sing to the tune of "Old MacDonald Had a Farm")

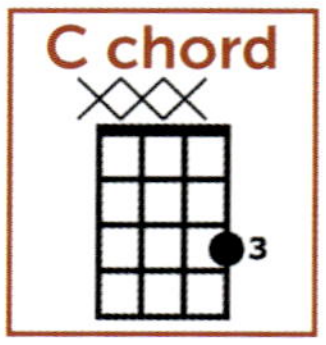

C (Strum down) C (Strum up)

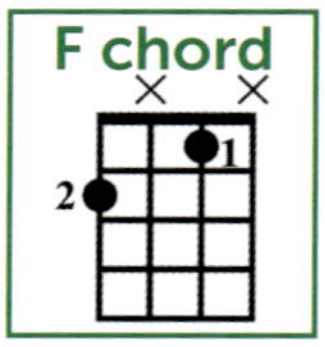

F (Strum down) F (Strum up)

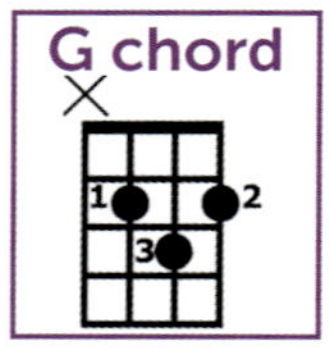

G (Strum down) G (Strum up)

Strum down

Strum up

C C C C F F C C

This young monk seal loved to bathe—

C C G G C C C C

E I E I O —— and

C C C C F F C C

in the bay he'd play all day ——

C C G G C C C

E I E I O ——

C C C C C C C C C C C C

With-a bark bark here and-a bark bark there

C C C F F F

Here a bark there a bark

C C C C C C C C

Eve - ry where a bark bark bark, Oh-

C C C C F F C C

This young monk seal loved to bathe—

C C G G C C C

E I E I O ——

Up-Down "Bounce" Strumming

Up-down strumming has a happy, bouncy feel!

It is like hopping or skipping, or singing a little song

in this rhythm: ta-TUM - ta-TUM - ta-TUM - ta-TUM

ta (UP) △

TUM (DOWN) ▼

So the rhythm is Up △ Down ▼, Up △ Down ▼, Up △ Down ▼.

Strum and sing **AND** for the **Up**-strum, and **NUMBER** for the **Down**-strum.

Like this:

and △- One ▼, and △-Two ▼, and △-Three ▼, and △-Four ▼, and △

Once you are used to this, go to the next page to practice chords.

Strumming Chords Up Then Down

This page is to practice strumming chords first **UP** then **DOWN**.

Strumming each chord first 8 times, then do the same 6 times, then 4 times, then 3 times, then 2 times.

What is new is that you must do UP-DOWN strumming!

On the word **AND** strum **up** (the triangle points up)
and on each **NUMBER** strum **down** (the triangle points down)

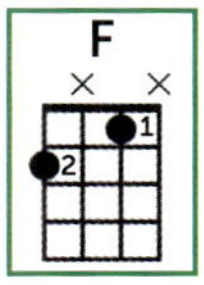

Start by strumming your F chord UP then Down rhythmically like saying ta-TUM - ta-TUM - ta-TUM - ta-TUM - ta-TUM - ta-TUM.

And 1 and 2 and 3 and 4 and 5 and 6 and 7 and 8

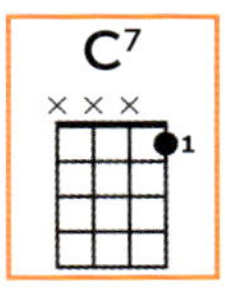

Now add the C^7 chord — ta-TUM - ta-TUM - ta-TUM.

And 1 and 2 and 3 and 4 and 5 and 6 and 7 and 8

Finish by strumming the F chord up and down.

And 1 and 2 and 3 and 4 and 5 and 6 and 7 and 8

Pūpū Hinuhinu   WINONA BEAMER

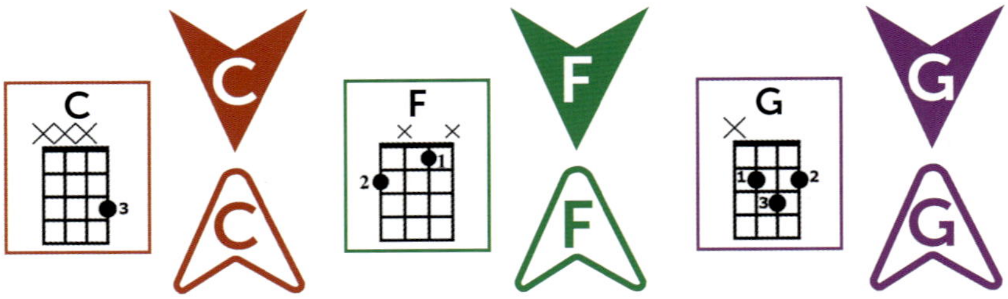

Strum down

Strum up

C C C C C C C C

Pū - pū ——— hi - nu hi - nu ———,

C C C C C F F G G G

Pū - pū ——— hi - nu hi - nu e ———,

G G C C C G G G C C F

O - ke Ka - ha - kai Ka - ha - kai e ———,

F C C G G G G C C C

Pū —— pū —— hi - nu hi - nu e ———!

My shell, shiny shell, my shell, pretty little one.
I found it by the ocean, my shell, pretty little one.

Watch and listen to Paula Fuga and children singing this sweet song on Lanikai Beach. https://www.youtube.com/watch?v=lu30Ha2_cxl

Practice Bounce Rhythm for Honu Song

The bounce strum rhythm is like skipping with your hand!

It is a down-strum followed by an up-strum

The down is firmer and a tiny bit longer than the up-strum.

At first, try to strum a C chord counting like this:

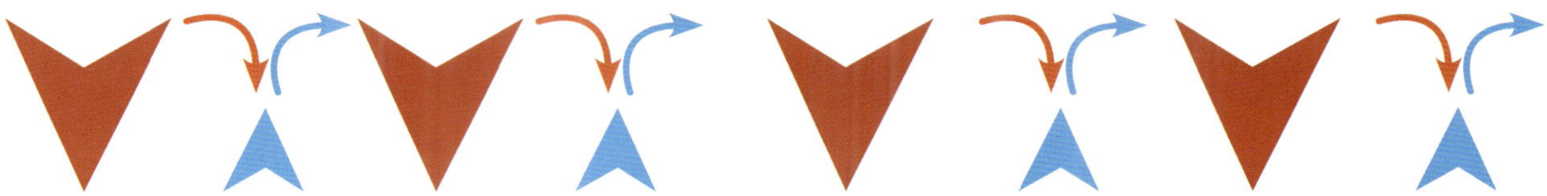

ONE and TWO and THREE and FOUR and

Keep strumming this pattern until the bounce is easy!

Now play each chord below, in the same rhythm, counting

ONE and TWO and THREE and FOUR for each chord.

Repat this until it is easy to "bounce" and change chords!

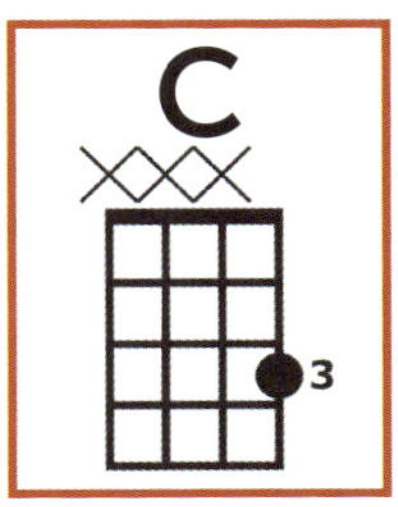

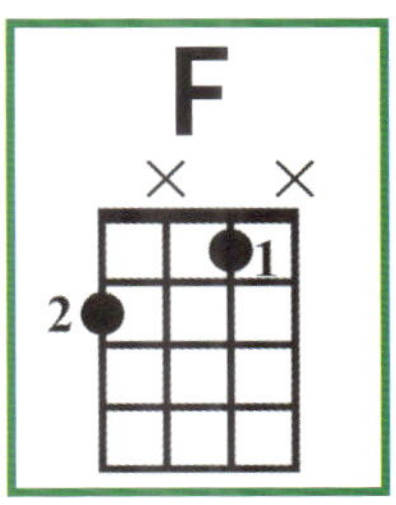

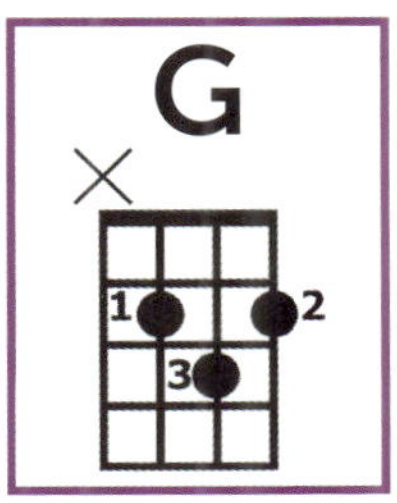

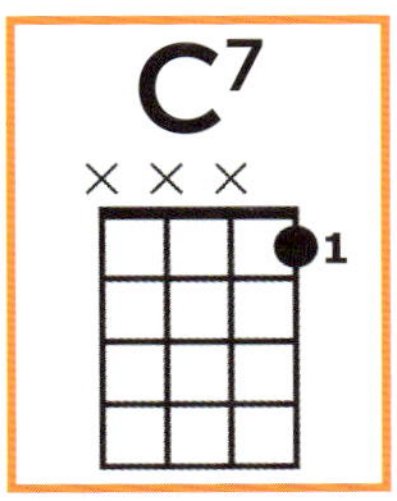

Honu Song
TRIA

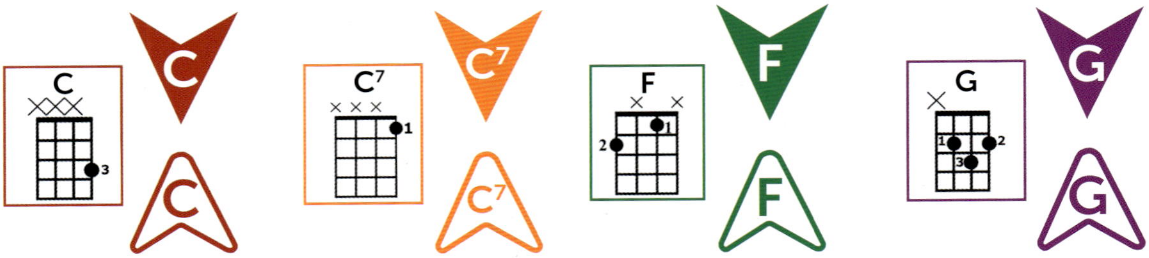

Ho - nu —, ho - nu —, ho – nu ————

Swim-ming in the sea ————,

Ho - nu —, ho - nu —, ho – nu ————,

C^7 C^7 C^7 C^7 C^7 C^7 C^7 C^7 F F F F F F F

Come and swim with me ——————

F G G G G G G G G G G G G

You're eat - ing fresh green li - mu ——————

G G G G G G G G C C C C C C

And the 'e - le —— 'e - le —— too! ——————

Listen to the "Honu Song" by Tria at this link:
https://www.youtube.com/watch?v=8ZZpSXsano0

Kōlea Song

(Sing to the tune of "Skip to My Lou.")

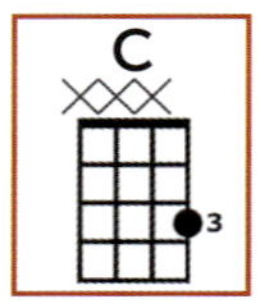

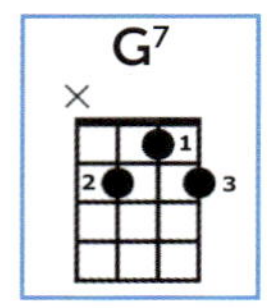

Strum down

Strum up

There's a lit-tle bird so wild and free —

Skip-ping and search- ing by the sea —

Sweet Kō - le - as so dain -ty and free —

Skip to Kō - le - a my dar — ling —

Chorus

Hey — ho — skip to Kō — le — a —

Hey — ho — skip to Kō — le — a —

Hey — ho — skip to Kō — le — a —

Skip to Kō - le - a my dar — ling —

Kō - le -a's her name so pret-ty and free ———

Near to the beach she will al - ways be ———

Skip-ping and search - ing by the sea ———

Skip to Kō- le - a my dar ——— ling ———

[Repeat Chorus]

Nai'a—Spinner Dolphin Song

(Sing to tune of "If You're Happy and You Know It Clap Your Hands.")

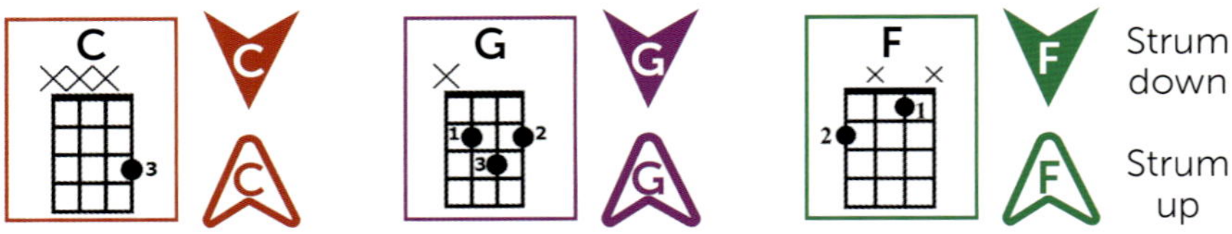

Spinner dolphin leaps and splashes full of glee ——

Spinner dolphin leaps and splashes full of glee ——

Spinner dolphin sails so free,

Leaping high a-bove the sea

She is calling join the fun and swim with me —— !

Happy Birthday Song

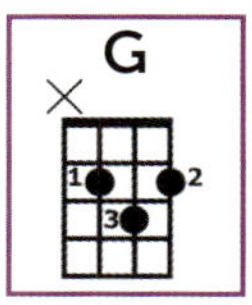

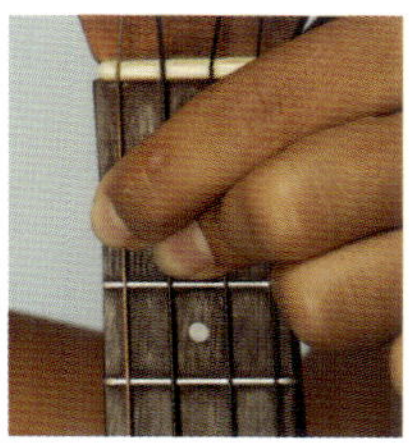

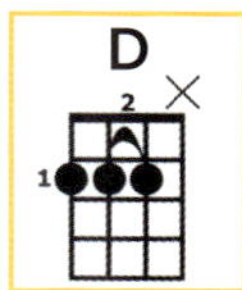

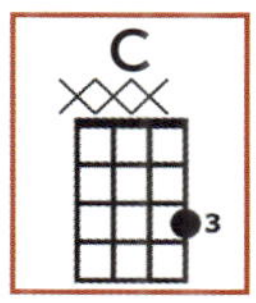

G G — D D — C C

Strum down

Strum up

G G G G G G G G D D D D D

Hap - py birth - day to you ———— !

D D D D D D D D G G G G G

Hap - py birth - day to you ———— !

G G G G G G G G D D C C C

Hap - py birth - day dear [name]

C C G G G G D D G G G G G G G

Hap - py birth - day to you ———— !

Playing New Chords: Am and E^7

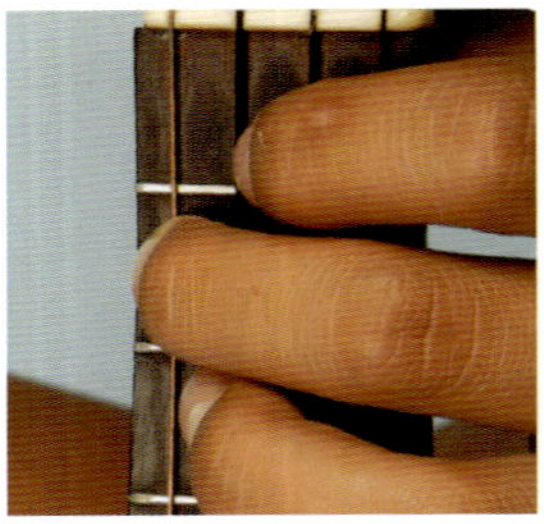

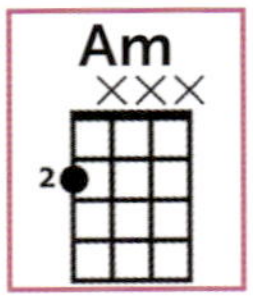

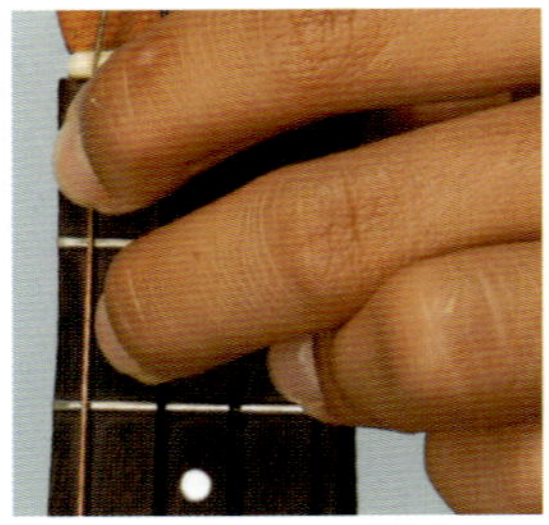

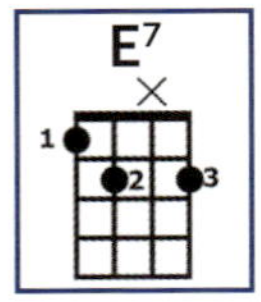

Strum down

Strum up

The A minor (Am) chord is very easy. It is played by pressing down **just your 2nd finger** on the 4th (G) string, 2nd fret. The other fingers in the photo are hovering above, not actually pressing down. Play as in the **Am** diagram.

The E^7 chord is played with three fingers. 1st finger on G string (1st fret), 2nd finger on C string (2nd fret). The 3rd finger is on the A string (also 2nd fret). It is a pretty chord.

1. First practice A minor chord eight times:
   Am, Am, Am, Am, Am, Am, Am, Am
   Then strum six times, then four times, then three times, then two times.

2. Do the same for E^7 chord eight times:
   E^7, E^7, E^7, E^7, E^7, E^7, E^7, E^7
   Then strum six times, then four times, then three times, then two times.

3. Practice the first lines of "Old King Cole" (Same tune for "The Song of King Kalākaua" on page 45.)

Old King Cole was a me - rry old— soul

And a mer - ry old— soul— was— he ——

The Song of King Kalākaua

(Sing to the tune of "Old King Cole")

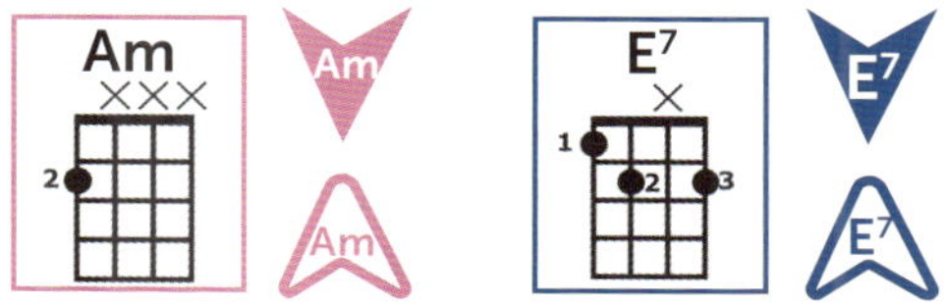

Strum down

Strum up

King Ka-lā-ka-ua was a me-rry monarch true,

And a ve -ry fine mon-arch was he ——— !

He— called for his sing-ers and he called for his i-pu

And he called for his 'u - ku - le— le ——— !

All his play-ers fine, sang and strummed in happy line,

Such a ve -ry fine group were they ——— !

There were none s-o rare, a-s could co - m - pare,

With our King and his 'u - ku - le - les fair ——— !

Aloha ʻOe (Chorus)
QUEEN LILIʻUOKALANI

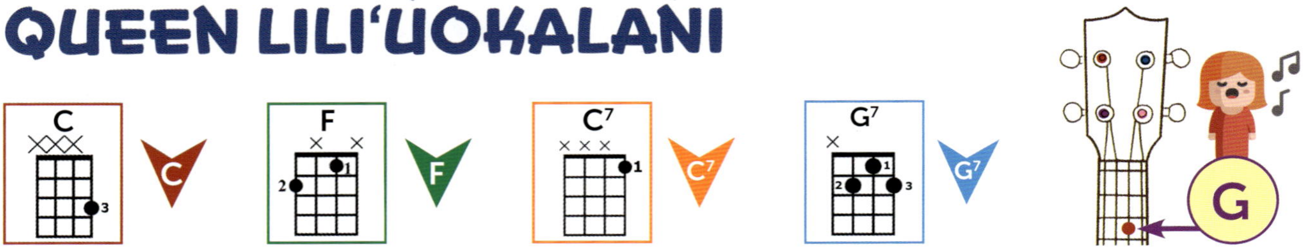

Watch Keiko Matsui:
https://www.youtube.com/watch?v=-8Sy3p1zYOY

The **Chorus** begins at 1:05 (1 minute and 5 seconds). You can strum along with Keiko if preferred. The strums here have been arranged to go with her singing.

A—lo— ha— ʻo-e—— a—lo—ha— ʻo-e—

E ke o - na - o - na no - ho i ka li——— po——

One fond em—brace—— a hoʻi aʻe au———

Un - til— we meet a-gain———

C7 F F F F F F F F C C C C C C C

A—lo— ha—— ʻoe—— a—lo—ha—— ʻoe——

C G7 G7 G7 G7 G7 G7 G7 G7 C C C C C7 C7 C7

E ke o - na - o - na no - ho i ka li——— po——

C7 F F F F F F F F C C C C C C C

One fond em—brace—— a hoʻi aʻe au——

C G7 G7 G7 G7 G7 G7 G7 G7 C C C C

Un - til— we meet a-gain——

C G7 G7 G7 G7 G7 G7 G7 G7 C C C C

Un - til— we meet a-gain——

Chords Used for Songs

C Chord, Down-strum

(pg. 21)

C

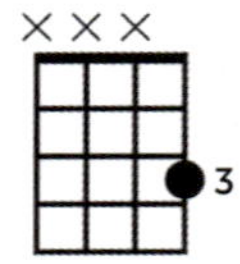

Twinkle, Twinkle, Little Star

(pg. 25)

C F G^7

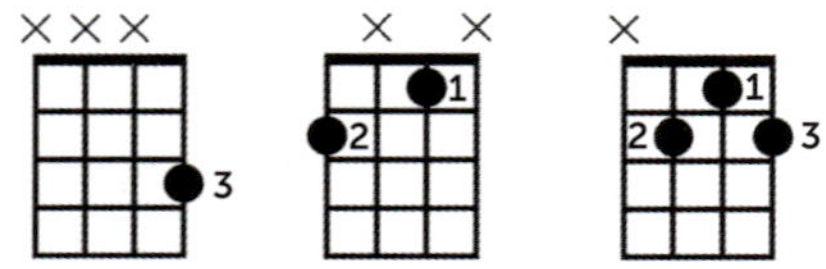

Nēnē Calling

(pg. 26)

C F G^7

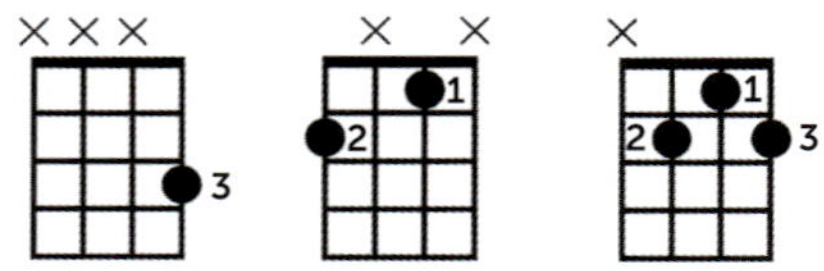

Pueo Song

(pg. 30)

F C^7

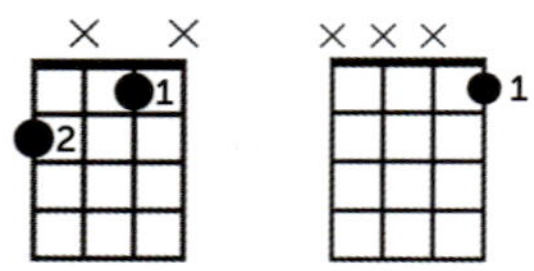

Hawaiian Monk Seal Song

(pg. 32)

C F G

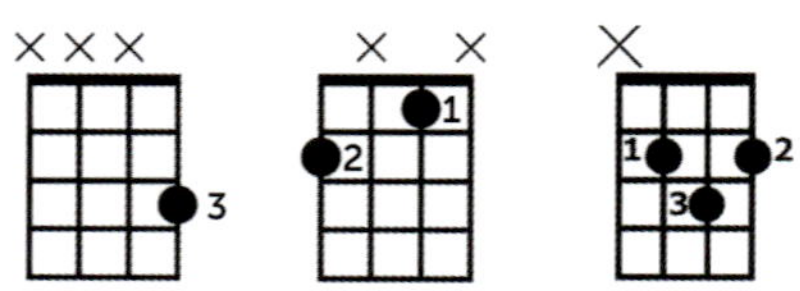

Pūpū Hinuhinu

(pg. 36)

C F G

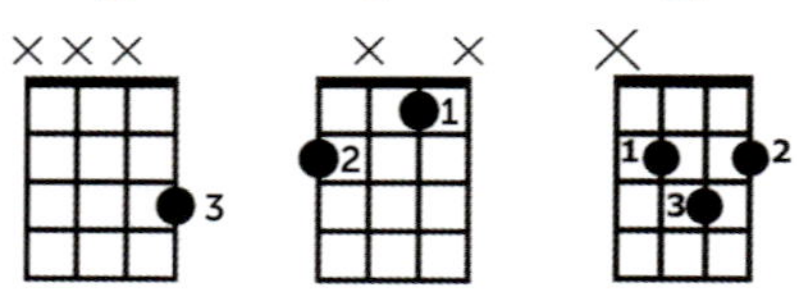

Honu Song

(pg. 38)

C C^7 F G

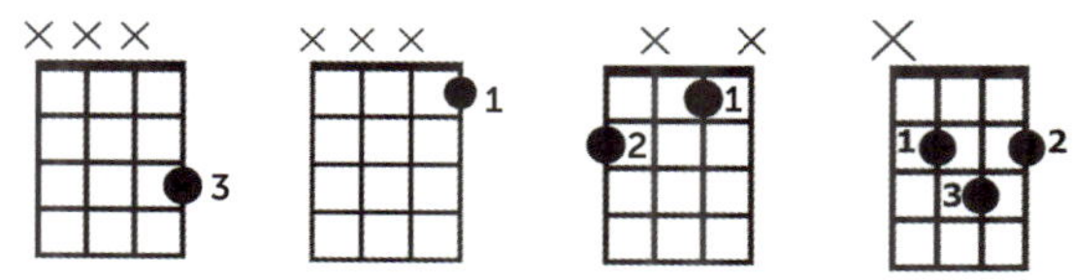

Kōlea Song

(pg. 40)

C G^7

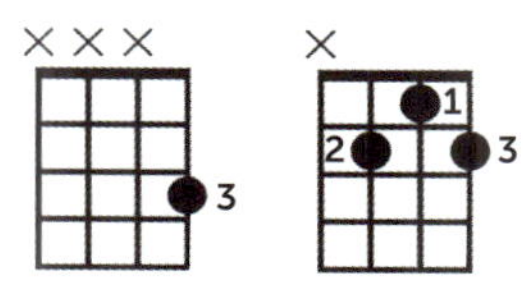

Naiʻa—Spinner Dolphin Song

(pg. 42)

C G F

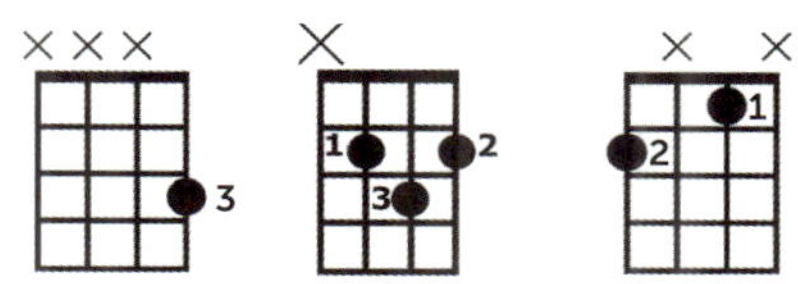

Happy Birthday Song

(pg. 43)

G D C

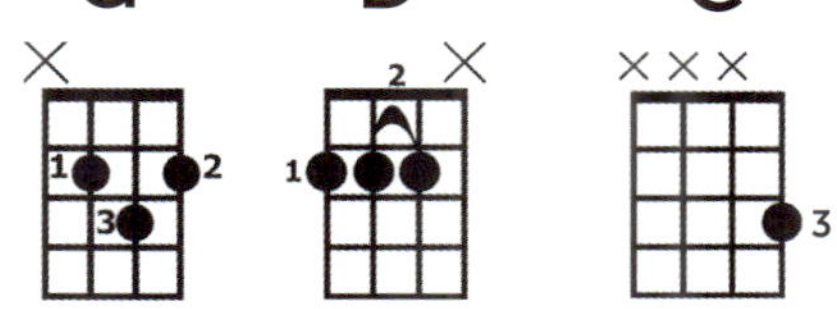

The Song of King Kalākaua

(pg. 45)

Am E^7

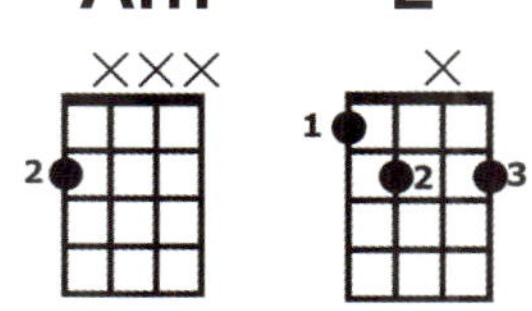

Aloha ʻOe

(pg. 46)

C F C^7 G^7

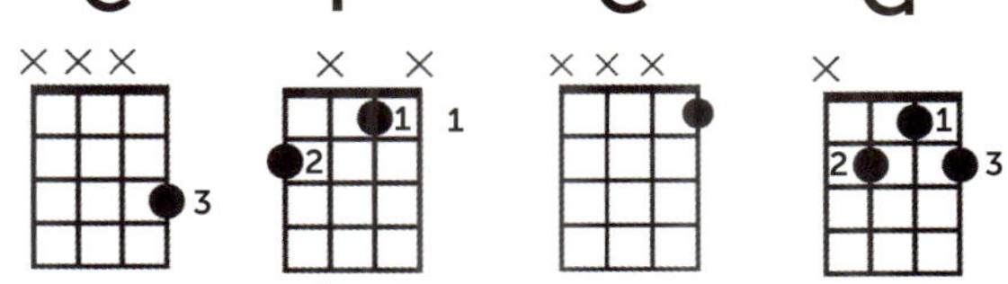

Scores for Hawaiian Songs

To parents, teachers, and other caregivers,

Almost all the melodies in this book are known to children.

However, unless you live in Hawai'i, the three Hawaiian songs may be unfamiliar.

For this reason, simple scores in the correct key, for Winona Beamer's song: "Pūpū Hinuhinu," Tria's Hawaiian Turtle song: "Honu," and the chorus of Queen Lili'uokalani's farewell song: "Aloha 'Oe," are added here.

If you prefer not to use Youtube to hear these songs' melodies and rhythms, the following scores can be sounded on a piano, recorder, or other melody instrument to give you a basic idea.

Pūpū Hinuhinu
WINONA BEAMER

With kind permission of Keola Beamer

Honu Song
TRIA

With kind permission of Tria

The Song of King Kalākaua

(Sing to the tune of "Old King Cole")

Aloha 'Oe (Chorus)
QUEEN LILI'UOKALANI

Tuning Your 'Ukulele

Most 'ukulele players use a small electronic tuner. This clips on the end of the 'ukulele and costs between $7.00 and $20.00.

'Ukulele Tuning

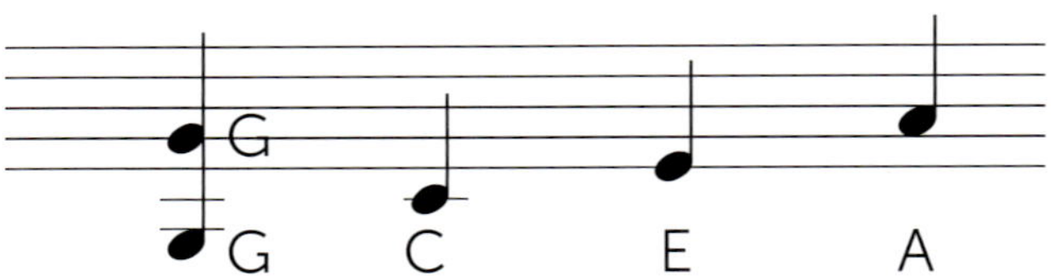

You can also tune from a piano, keyboard, or even by ear. When you are playing in a group always tune everyone to the reference (piano, etc.) not to each other, or like the Chinese whispers, the tuning can slowly change as you go along the line.

Birds and Sea Life in Hawai'i

Many creatures are unique to our Hawaiian Islands!

The **Nēnē** goose is exclusively found in the wild on the islands of O'ahu, Maui, Kaua'i, Moloka'i, and Hawai'i. In 1957, it was designated as the official bird of the state of Hawai'i.

The **Pueo**, or short-eared owl, is also native to Hawai'i. In Hawaiian culture it is regarded as an 'aumakua or spirit ancestor and guardian.

The Pacific Golden Plover called **Kōlea** in Hawai'i, is found on or near beaches often running on the sands. At the end of summer, it flies all the way from Alaska to live on the shores of the Hawaiian islands.

The Hawaiian **monk seal** is found only in the Hawaiian Islands. It is native to the islands, occurring nowhere else in the world.

The Hawaiian spinner dolphin is smaller than the regular dolphins and it is known for spinning or flipping as it leaps out of the sea! The Hawaiian word for these dolphins is **Nai'a**.

Honu is the name of our beloved and gentle Hawaiian green sea turtle. They are often found swimming and feeding by rocks and reefs.

About the Author

Michael Preston was born in Uganda and attended elementary school in Kenya. His family later immigrated to New Zealand. After high school he worked for a year as a volunteer in Vanuatu where he discovered his passion for ʻukulele while playing with the local people. Later, when he moved to Hawaiʻi as a teacher, his passion for ʻukulele was reignited as he followed many Hawaiian performing groups and took lessons with local musicians. His love of Hawaiian and international music led him to develop an approach to teaching ʻukulele that was enthusiastically adopted by many students during his fifteen years as a teacher in Honolulu.

During this time, Preston developed an approach to learning ʻukulele that was easy to follow, helping build the right skills at the right pace.

This led to his collaboration with Mutual Publishing to write several ʻukulele books. The first was for beginners: *Let's Kanikapila! Ten Steps to Learn ʻUkulele the Hawaiian Way.* In collaboration with Mutual Publishing, he went on to write three further ʻukulele instruction books.

In 2006, Preston and his wife, a preschool teacher, moved to Seattle and later to Bellingham. He has continued to teach ʻukulele and arrange music for players of all ages. He and his wife have three adult children and eight grandchildren.